Published by:
SPURBOOKS LTD.,
6 Parade Court,
Bourne End,
Buckinghamshire.

Sketch maps by Mike Pocock

...publication all the walks in this book were
...is designated as official footpaths, but it should
...nd that deviation orders may be made from

ISBN 0 904978 07 9

...d by Maund & Irvine, Tring, Herts.

Walk

VE

SPURBOO

Contents

(10) Pangbourne
Pangbourne Meadow, Mapledurham Lock, Purley.
—5½ miles.

(11) Pangbourne
Sulham Woods, Long Lane, Tidmarsh, River Pang.—
5½ miles.

(12) Bucklebury Common
Turners Green, The Slade, Upper Common, Hopwoods Green.—5 miles.

(13) Bucklebury Common
Lower Common, Redhill Copse, Bucklebury, Pangfold Farm, Chapel Row.—7 miles.

(14) Bucklebury Common
Lower Common, Midgham, Midgham Park, Carbins Wood.—3½ miles.

(15) West Ilsley
Ridgeway, Bury Down, Sheep Down (N.W. of W. Ilsley).—4½ miles.

(16) East Ilsley
Ridgeway, Sheep Down (N.E. of W. Ilsley), Gore Hill, Hodcott Down, Yewtree Hill.—5 miles.

(17) Compton
Roden Downs, Ridgeway, Compton Downs.—4½ miles.

(18) Hungerford
Through farmland and open country to Standen Manor and back.—4 miles.

(19) Hungerford
Hungerford Common, Templeton, Dun Mill Lock.—4 miles.

(20) Kintbury
Kennet and Avon Canal, Titcomb Manor, Mount Pleasant, Kintbury Crossways.—3½ miles.

Introduction

Berkshire, more compact than it once was, is a county of infinite variety, and there is no better way of discovering its rural charm than to get off the highways and out on the paths and byways. If you want to know more about this beautiful county can I recommend 'Companion into Berkshire' by R. P. Beckinsale and 'The Thames Valley' by Frank Martin, both published by Spurbooks.

This selection of walks travels from east to west; from the meadow paths beside the Thames around Pangbourne and Cookham, through the wooded commonland near Newbury, and over the more remote downland where the ancient Ridgeway journeys above the villages of Compton and the Ilsleys.

Parking space is available at all the given starting points, and where there is suitable public transport details are given, though it is wise to check that there have been no further cuts or changes.

One of the joys of walking is that no walk is ever the same twice over, it varies according to the month, the weather, the time of day. So in calling these walks for all ages and all seasons, may I add that where we have discovered a route to be particularly enjoyable at any one time of the year, I have mentioned it in the text.

Happy walking!

V.B.

Abbreviations

    P.F. Public Footpath.

    P.F. & B. Public Footpath and bridleway.

    W.A. White arrow.

Please observe the Countryside Code.

Cookham

**Beside the Thames, Cockmarsh,
Terry's Lane, The Moor.
4 miles**

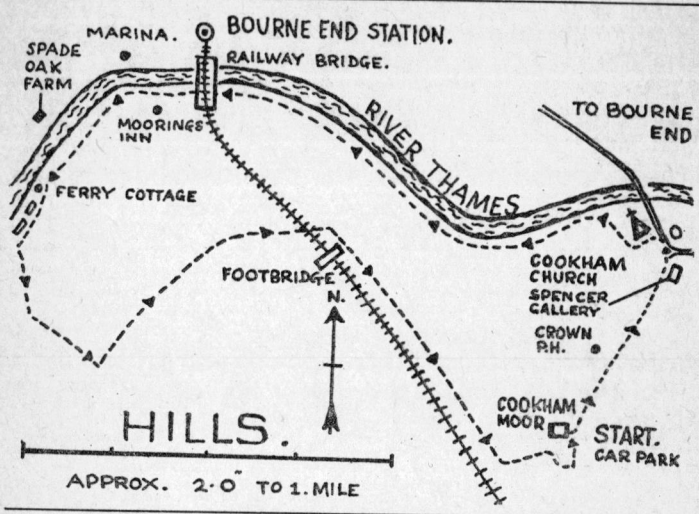

This first walk is one which I can safely recommend for anyone who might be out of practice, or unused to walking far. The paths are firm, with virtually no uphill work, and they ask to be enjoyed at a leisurely pace with pauses to watch whatever activity there is on the river. There is even a strategically placed pub part-way round. Moreover, it is an attractive and varied outing, partly on Trust land with both pastoral and river scenery.

How to get there—By car to car park on The Moor, west of Cookham village.

By train—To Cookham and ¼ mile walk to The Moor.

By bus—The Thames Valley 20 Windsor-High Wycombe. Alight in Sutton Road by Stanley Spencer Gallery. Pick up walk at (A).

From the National Trust car park on The Moor walk towards the village, and up the High Street between the definitely old-world buildings, passing in order of sequence, the Crown, Royal Exchange, the Bee and the Dragon, and the Stanley Spencer Gallery.

Sir Stanley Spencer, who lived and worked in Cookham for most of his life, portrayed the village over and over again in his paintings. The Gallery opens throughout the year.

(A) Beyond the Gallery turn left as signposted to Bourne End, seeing, across the road, the Tarry Stone, a massive lump of rugged stone, the starting point of the village sports in medieval days. Almost immediately beyond it turn left past Churchgate, the picturesque entry to the church grounds. Follow the gravel path to pass the 850-year-old church right, and at far side go via a kissing-gate to reach the bank of the Thames.

Turn left along the river bank. Very soon the residential district is left behind, and once through a gate pastureland extends to left. Just keep to path, and after encountering two more gates find a group of hollow willows lining the way.

Once past willows go under a railway bridge, and on as riverside chalets appear. The next landmark is The Moorings inn, and the Bourne End Marina is in sight on the opposite bank. Continue ahead past all the chalets till another gate ushers you to Cockmarsh, the Trust-owned part of the wide flat plain extending along this southern bank.

Still stay with the riverside path, going through yet another gate and, just after noting the historic farm at Spade Oak on the far bank, arrive at Ferry Cottage; regrettably, the ferry no longer operates.

From here the route, about to turn back to Cookham, gradually strays away from the water. Follow the path, bearing left and round the back of Ferry Cottage, to then walk alongside the rear of a further group of chalets till path bends left again to a P.F. sign. Go past sign and forward across field towards the rising hillside. At far side of field climb stile to be greeted by an inviting array of paths. But because this set out to be a level walk, our route goes forward for a few yards, then directly left on a well defined broad track rounding the foot of the hillside.

When finally this exceedingly pleasant track meets a high stile, cross and keep straight on. On nearing the railway tunnel bear right towards a wide pair of gates, but short of them turn left and through the tunnel to discover a P.F. sign. Here climb stile to right, go up the steps and follow path to reach the new golf course. Then turn right, keeping to path with course left and railway off to right. Soon path climbs slightly and arrives at a bridge. Do not cross, but carry on bearing fractionally left, i.e. veering away from railway.

On reaching corner of field still carry on, wire fence right. When wooden stile is met, cross, and a few steps down drive arrive at road by a house, Fiveways.

Turn left for only a pace or so to go across road to a stile opposite leading into field. Use fieldpath hugging left-hand hedge, thus walking parallel with road. At bottom go via gap to road, Terry's Lane, and then right to shortly arrive at the main road into Cookham. Turn left to return to The Moor.

Refreshments   Copper Kettle, Two Roses, Cookham—many inns in village.

Cookham

**The Moor, Gravel Pit, Strand Water.
4 miles.**

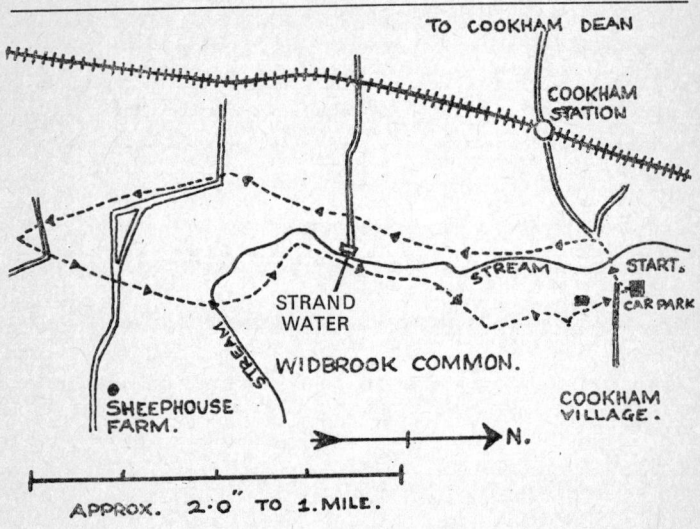

This is a meadow walk enlivened by local springs and streams, where flowering rushes, water lilies and white arrowhead embroider the water, and tall spikes of purple loosestrife colour the banks. Look out for waterfowl as well, coot, heron, moorhen, and, near the gravel pit, parties of Canada geese. Suitable all year round, but at its best in spring and summer.

How to get there—By car or train as Walk 1.

By bus—Alight in Sutton Road at Stanley Spencer Gallery and walk down village street and on over The Moor to the National Trust car park.

From National Trust car park on The Moor turn right along road, and when The Moor ends go left across road to follow

11

signposted footpath leading over stile, and along meadow to second stile. Path continues with field left, garden right, and after next stile follow meadow path straight on to climb half-obscured stile in far corner. Still forward, row of silver willows off to left, to reach a wide crossing track. Go over it, veering right and continuing forward with hedge right.

At far side reach metal gate, and beyond it go ahead to next stile where walk over gravel drive to a footpath sign pointing the way you have come. Straight on, again veering slightly right on distinct path bisecting meadowland. On arrival at stile right, ignore, and keep forward over footbridge, and along top of bank, course of stream to left. The next landmark is a further footbridge on your left.

(At this point if you wish to curtail the walk, use the footbridge and walk on a few yards to reach Strand Water and pick up the return to Cookham from (A).

The main 4 mile route is simply forward by left edge of field till stile leads to a gravel track. Follow this track only till it bends left, then desert it to climb metal stile and regain the meadows. Bear slightly right over grass to an obvious stile, cross, continue to next and yet another gravel track. Walk across it to follow unmistakable grass path eventually taking you towards a further footbridge.

Stop just short of bridge, and turn very sharp left, thus making a V turn and re-crossing meadow to leave it at its far corner, where you will find four tracks meet. The converted gravel pit is now in view. From here take the forward, fenced path, so that the water, and possibly yachts, are behind you.

When this path ends, and private drives lead off to either side, use metal stile facing you and follow field-path, fence right.

On the meadows here we have seen as many as a hundred Canada geese.

The next stile is a stout one, and beyond it go ahead over wooden footbridge, and on in line with left-hand hedge. Climb next stile, forward on narrower path to the stage at which metal fencing right ceases.

(A) Here turn sharp right (or sharp left if you are following short route) under willow and along path bordered by the fertile banks of Strand Water left, whilst fields extend on the other side. On reaching a lane, running crossways, walk over and bear right to stile and on along left edge of field to a further stile. Climb, and walk on less wide, but well defined path. Straightforwardly it leads you to emerge in Cookham by Moor Hall, from which point the return to the car park is obvious.

Refreshments See Walk 1.

signposted footpath leading over stile, and along meadow to second stile. Path continues with field left, garden right, and after next stile follow meadow path straight on to climb half-obscured stile in far corner. Still forward, row of silver willows off to left, to reach a wide crossing track. Go over it, veering right and continuing forward with hedge right.

At far side reach metal gate, and beyond it go ahead to next stile where walk over gravel drive to a footpath sign pointing the way you have come. Straight on, again veering slightly right on distinct path bisecting meadowland. On arrival at stile right, ignore, and keep forward over footbridge, and along top of bank, course of stream to left. The next landmark is a further footbridge on your left.

(At this point if you wish to curtail the walk, use the footbridge and walk on a few yards to reach Strand Water and pick up the return to Cookham from (A).

The main 4 mile route is simply forward by left edge of field till stile leads to a gravel track. Follow this track only till it bends left, then desert it to climb metal stile and regain the meadows. Bear slightly right over grass to an obvious stile, cross, continue to next and yet another gravel track. Walk across it to follow unmistakable grass path eventually taking you towards a further footbridge.

Stop just short of bridge, and turn very sharp left, thus making a V turn and re-crossing meadow to leave it at its far corner, where you will find four tracks meet. The converted gravel pit is now in view. From here take the forward, fenced path, so that the water, and possibly yachts, are behind you.

When this path ends, and private drives lead off to either side, use metal stile facing you and follow field-path, fence right.

On the meadows here we have seen as many as a hundred Canada geese.

The next stile is a stout one, and beyond it go ahead over wooden footbridge, and on in line with left-hand hedge. Climb next stile, forward on narrower path to the stage at which metal fencing right ceases.

(A) Here turn sharp right (or sharp left if you are following

Cookham

**The Moor, Gravel Pit, Strand Water.
4 miles.**

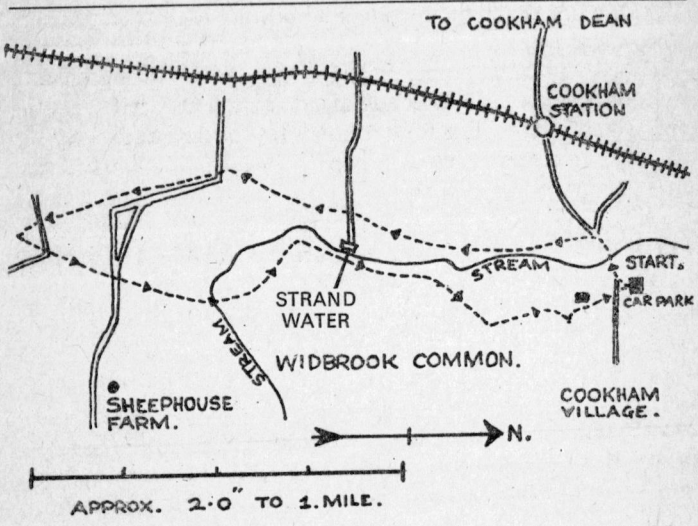

This is a meadow walk enlivened by local springs and streams, where flowering rushes, water lilies and white arrowhead embroider the water, and tall spikes of purple loosestrife colour the banks. Look out for waterfowl as well, coot, heron, moorhen, and, near the gravel pit, parties of Canada geese. Suitable all year round, but at its best in spring and summer.

How to get there—By car or train as Walk 1.

By bus—Alight in Sutton Road at Stanley Spencer Gallery and walk down village street and on over The Moor to the National Trust car park.

From National Trust car park on The Moor turn right along road, and when The Moor ends go left across road to follow then directly left on a well defined broad track rounding the foot of the hillside.

When finally this exceedingly pleasant track meets a high stile, cross and keep straight on. On nearing the railway tunnel bear right towards a wide pair of gates, but short of them turn left and through the tunnel to discover a P.F. sign. Here climb stile to right, go up the steps and follow path to reach the new golf course. Then turn right, keeping to path with course left and railway off to right. Soon path climbs slightly and arrives at a bridge. Do not cross, but carry on bearing fractionally left, i.e. veering away from railway.

On reaching corner of field still carry on, wire fence right. When wooden stile is met, cross, and a few steps down drive arrive at road by a house, Fiveways.

Turn left for only a pace or so to go across road to a stile opposite leading into field. Use fieldpath hugging left-hand hedge, thus walking parallel with road. At bottom go via gap to road, Terry's Lane, and then right to shortly arrive at the main road into Cookham. Turn left to return to The Moor.

Refreshments   Copper Kettle, Two Roses, Cookham—many inns in village.

From the National Trust car park on The Moor walk towards the village, and up the High Street between the definitely old-world buildings, passing in order of sequence, the Crown, Royal Exchange, the Bee and the Dragon, and the Stanley Spencer Gallery.

Sir Stanley Spencer, who lived and worked in Cookham for most of his life, portrayed the village over and over again in his paintings. The Gallery opens throughout the year.

(A) Beyond the Gallery turn left as signposted to Bourne End, seeing, across the road, the Tarry Stone, a massive lump of rugged stone, the starting point of the village sports in medieval days. Almost immediately beyond it turn left past Churchgate, the picturesque entry to the church grounds. Follow the gravel path to pass the 850-year-old church right, and at far side go via a kissing-gate to reach the bank of the Thames.

Turn left along the river bank. Very soon the residential district is left behind, and once through a gate pastureland extends to left. Just keep to path, and after encountering two more gates find a group of hollow willows lining the way.

Once past willows go under a railway bridge, and on as riverside chalets appear. The next landmark is The Moorings inn, and the Bourne End Marina is in sight on the opposite bank. Continue ahead past all the chalets till another gate ushers you to Cockmarsh, the Trust-owned part of the wide flat plain extending along this southern bank.

Still stay with the riverside path, going through yet another gate and, just after noting the historic farm at Spade Oak on the far bank, arrive at Ferry Cottage; regrettably, the ferry no longer operates.

From here the route, about to turn back to Cookham, gradually strays away from the water. Follow the path, bearing left and round the back of Ferry Cottage, to then walk alongside the rear of a further group of chalets till path bends left again to a P.F. sign. Go past sign and forward across field towards the rising hillside. At far side of field climb stile to be greeted by an inviting array of paths. But because this set out to be a level walk, our route goes forward for a few yards,

Cookham

**Beside the Thames, Cockmarsh,
Terry's Lane, The Moor.
4 miles**

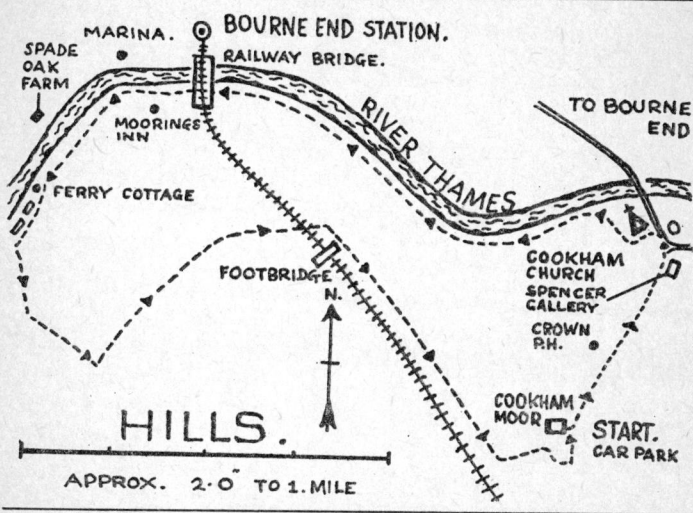

This first walk is one which I can safely recommend for anyone who might be out of practice, or unused to walking far. The paths are firm, with virtually no uphill work, and they ask to be enjoyed at a leisurely pace with pauses to watch whatever activity there is on the river. There is even a strategically placed pub part-way round. Moreover, it is an attractive and varied outing, partly on Trust land with both pastoral and river scenery.

How to get there—By car to car park on The Moor, west of Cookham village.

By train—To Cookham and ¼ mile walk to The Moor.

By bus—The Thames Valley 20 Windsor-High Wycombe. Alight in Sutton Road by Stanley Spencer Gallery. Pick up walk at (A).

Introduction

Berkshire, more compact than it once was, is a county of infinite variety, and there is no better way of discovering its rural charm than to get off the highways and out on the paths and byways. If you want to know more about this beautiful county can I recommend 'Companion into Berkshire' by R. P. Beckinsale and 'The Thames Valley' by Frank Martin, both published by Spurbooks.

This selection of walks travels from east to west; from the meadow paths beside the Thames around Pangbourne and Cookham, through the wooded commonland near Newbury, and over the more remote downland where the ancient Ridgeway journeys above the villages of Compton and the Ilsleys.

Parking space is available at all the given starting points, and where there is suitable public transport details are given, though it is wise to check that there have been no further cuts or changes.

One of the joys of walking is that no walk is ever the same twice over, it varies according to the month, the weather, the time of day. So in calling these walks for all ages and all seasons, may I add that where we have discovered a route to be particularly enjoyable at any one time of the year, I have mentioned it in the text.

Happy walking!

V.B.

Abbreviations

    P.F. Public Footpath.

    P.F. & B. Public Footpath and bridleway.

    W.A. White arrow.

Please observe the Countryside Code.

(10) Pangbourne

Pangbourne Meadow, Mapledurham Lock, Purley.
—5½ miles.

(11) Pangbourne

Sulham Woods, Long Lane, Tidmarsh, River Pang.—
5½ miles.

(12) Bucklebury Common

Turners Green, The Slade, Upper Common, Hopwoods Green.—5 miles.

(13) Bucklebury Common

Lower Common, Redhill Copse, Bucklebury, Pangfold Farm, Chapel Row.—7 miles.

(14) Bucklebury Common

Lower Common, Midgham, Midgham Park, Carbins
Wood.—3½ miles.

(15) West Ilsley

Ridgeway, Bury Down, Sheep Down (N.W. of W.
Ilsley).—4½ miles.

(16) East Ilsley

Ridgeway, Sheep Down (N.E. of W. Ilsley), Gore
Hill, Hodcott Down, Yewtree Hill.—5 miles.

(17) Compton

Roden Downs, Ridgeway, Compton Downs.—4½
miles.

(18) Hungerford

Through farmland and open country to Standen
Manor and back.—4 miles.

(19) Hungerford

Hungerford Common, Templeton, Dun Mill Lock.—
4 miles.

(20) Kintbury

Kennet and Avon Canal, Titcomb Manor, Mount
Pleasant, Kintbury Crossways.—3½ miles.

Contents

Introduction

Maidenhead Thicket

**Pinkneys Green, Hindhay Farm.
4 miles.**

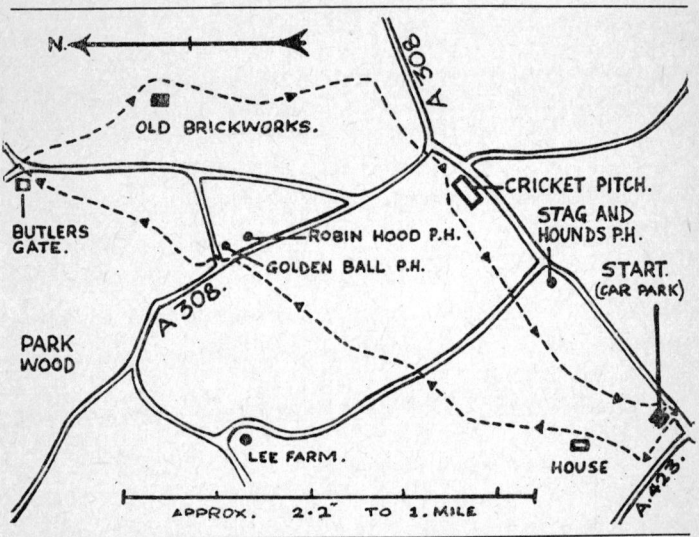

One of the advantages of footpaths within easy reach of habitation is that they are invariably unobstructed and well trodden, and suitable for walking whatever the time of year. This certainly applies to a walk around the area west of Maidenhead, where there are several pockets of green, thicket and rough pasturage, once the haunt of highwaymen, and now belonging to the National Trust.

How to get there—By car to the Maidenhead Thicket National Trust car park, reached by turning off the A423 and a few yards along Pinkneys Drive.

By bus—Alder Valley 18, Maidenhead to Marlow. Alight at the Golden Ball, Pinkneys Green, from which stage pick up walk at (A).

Walk out of car park and turn right along grass verge of Pinkneys Drive for nearly 100 yards. Then turn right on very clear grass ride through the Thicket. After 200 yards emerge from Thicket and turn right along broad expanse of turf. After 250 yards on reaching house, Leigh Cottage, left, bear left by low railings to road. Keep ahead along it, more houses soon developing, and immediately past Pinkneys Court, left, arrive at a meeting of lanes.

Still ahead, on No Through Road facing you. When you reach St. Timothee (sic) go straight on by means of a green path soon going between concrete posts, and clearly continuing forward at edge of farmland. Once past more posts it reverts to a drive leading to road, near a National Trust Pinkneys Green sign. The Robin Hood is seen right, but our route is 50 yards left along road to bus stop opposite Golden Ball Lane.

(A) From the bus stop cross road, and a few yards down Golden Ball Lane, and opposite the inn of the same name, turn left on further drive to Fairwinds and Treetops only. Having passed both these houses, drive peters out to a footpath. When it forks keep left and forward beside edge of copse. Stay with your path, and on it re-dividing follow forward, ignoring all side tracks, and eventually, towards end of copse, bear right to road.

Turn left to road junction and obvious P.F. sign opposite house, Butlers Gate. Turn right, and back as it were, on path heading for wood, as the P.F. sign points. At division of path use left fork, and near end of wood, on meeting wooden fence, bear slightly left through a squeeze stile, and on to reach open country, and a stile. Cross, turn right along field edge to climb further stile by P.F. sign.

Walk ahead across yard of Hindhay Farm to a 2-armed P.F. sign. Take the path still ahead over stile, and a second, by gate, to carry on first beneath a row of trees, and then straight on to obvious stile, as Maidenhead appears in the distance. Once beyond next stile bear diagonally right over rough field in the direction of farm outbuildings to find two P.F. signs. Turn right over stile, or through adjoining gate, and along fenced path, developing to driveway. As it winds left towards road, leave and keep forward over grass to P.F. sign to Cookham Dean.

Here, walk along Pinkneys Drive, before you, for 70 yards to meet copse, and bear right to go round it. You are now, of course, on Pinkneys Green. On seeing a fine, single sweet chestnut stay to right of that too, and passing cricket pitch left follow round next copse. Pass right of a lone maple tree, and then forwards towards houses; aim at a group of easily seen white posts backed by a wooden fence. When edge of Green is reached, cross road, pass the aforesaid posts, and forward to walk between some more posts and along distinct track. Then on over grass to next narrow road, cross, and keep your direction to visible gap into Thicket, i.e. not wider ride slightly right of your path. Once on the Thicket path it will return you directly to the car park.

Refreshments   Golden Ball, and Robin Hood *en route*, Stag and Hounds, Pinkneys Green.

Hurley

**Towpath, Hallplace Farm,
Prospect Hill, Hurley Bottom.
5 miles.**

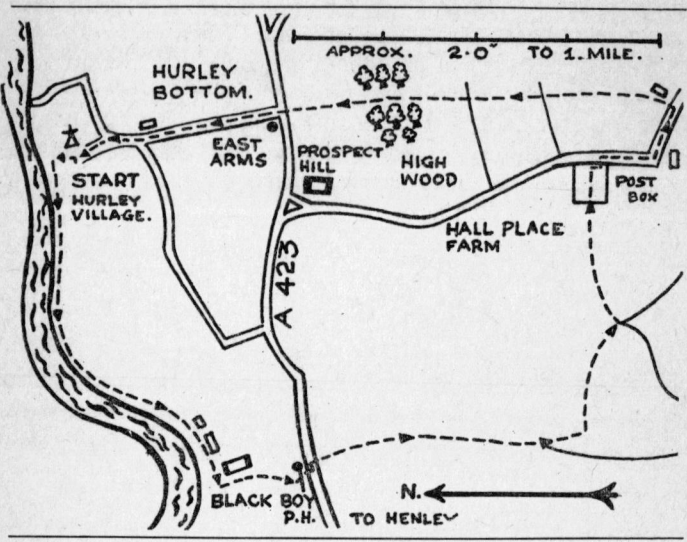

The Thames adds interest to the beginning of this walk. It then turns away from the river along undisturbed country paths in which the botanist will take particular delight, and climbs almost imperceptibly to the top of Prospect Hill. And if Hurley is unknown to you, do leave time to stroll around the historic village where, about 1,000 years ago, Benedictine monks built a monastery.

How to get there—By car to car park at northern end of village by church.

By bus—Alder Valley, Henley—Maidenhead, and South Midland Coach, London-Oxford. Alight by East Arms at southern end of village. Pick up walk at (A)—that is almost at the end!

Walk out of the car park to immediately turn left on P.F. marked 'No cycling'. It leads past The Tithe Barn, a decorative house—Hurley specialises in such houses. Very shortly arrive at steps. Go up, and then, at P.F. sign, turn sharp left along tow-path, that is **do not** cross bridge over river. Within a matter of yards go through gate, over steps beside a boathouse, and after that stay with the tow-path as it broadens out.

You will pass through a gate, and on approaching a white cottage continue past it and a row of riverside chalets over-shadowed by lofty pines. Beyond next gate path is replaced by gravelled drive. Ignore P.F. off left between houses, and after 100 yards reach road. Turn left along it.

Deserting the river now, there is open country all around. Pass Frogmill Farm left, and continue to main road, by the Black Boy. Cross carefully—it is a fast road—turn left for only a few steps, then right up a P.F. There should be a sign marking the way. Overhung by elm and hawthorn initially, the way soon clears. Climbing imperceptibly the single file path is bordered by a glorious confusion of wild flowers.

At the top brief gaps in right-hand bushrow allow pastoral views. When a group of varied signs is met, go left on bridle-way as to Honey Lane. For a short distance only the way travels through a woodland reserve of the Bucks, Berks and Oxon Naturalists' Trust. But our route quite quickly emerges through a gate into meadowland.

Go straight ahead, with longer views of sheep grazing in the neat experimental enclosures of the Grassland Research Institute, which owns 600 acres of farmland hereabouts on which it has been carrying out research since 1948.

Once through a gateway meet a concrete track. Now do not go left, but carry on down, so that fields are still right. At bottom, with double wooden gate right, turn left along farm drive, passing and disregarding P.F. right. Soon go through wide gate, and onwards to Hallplace Farm. Make your way through the farmyard, as clear signs direct, and then turn right along the quiet road.

At the top, post-box facing you, turn left for about 200 yards.

Now, just short of Ladyplace Cottages, turn abruptly left over stile. The P.F. sign is inclined to be hidden in the gap in the hedge. Carry on across meadow following round the right edge, under several sturdy oaks, till a stile is met. Climb, and speedily over a second one to an extensive cultivated field. Straight ahead to a 2-armed P.F. sign on further side of field, and stile to a narrow drive. A stile facing you ushers you back to grassland, and there, in the distance, are the Chiltern hills rising out of the deep valley of the Thames.

When next drive and P.F. sign are encountered, keep forward towards High Wood. Enter wood by stile to follow woodland track, initially between lush undergrowth and then through a dappled beech glade. At far side a stile acts as exit and the prelude to a breath-taking Chiltern view from the summit of the aptly named Prospect Hill. Closer at hand, the red roofs of Hurley cluster below, and to the left is the plain brick building of the Grassland Research Institute.

A slim pathway hurries down the steep hill.

(A) On arrival at road by the East Arms, cross and go down road opposite, to Hurley ½ mile. By walking straight on down through the village, past the universally acclaimed Old Bell, and the Monk's Barn dating from A.D. 1100, you will return to the car park.

Refreshments   Tea-rooms Marlow and Henley. Black Boy, East Arms, Old Bell all met on way.

Honey Lane near Burchetts Green

**Ashley Hill Woods, Warren Row, Hallplace Farm.
4 miles.**

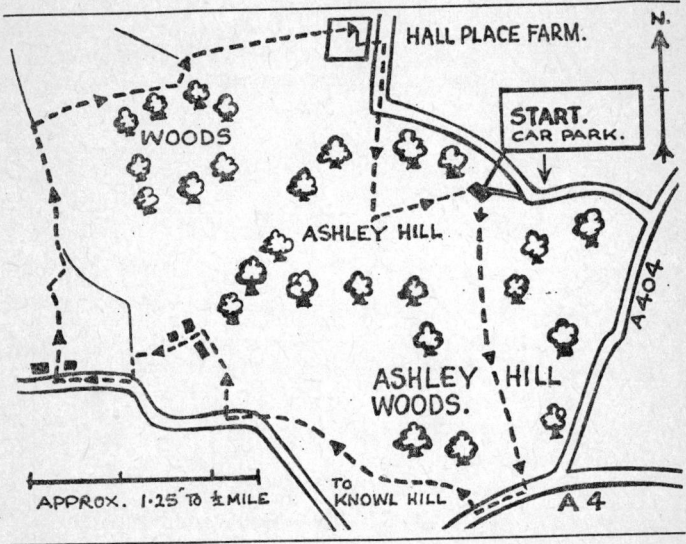

Starting off through a delightful stretch of Forestry Commission land, with mixed deciduous and evergreen trees and wide flower-strewn rides, this route moves on to meadowland, encounters a pub, and also passes by some of the fields of the Grassland Research Farm. The peaceful and varied paths make it a first rate all-seasons walk.

How to get there—By car to the Forestry Commission car park in Honey Lane, just off the A404.

At the car park entrance see a P.F. sign guiding you up and through the pedestrian passway to Ashley Hill Woods, a part of Bramshill Forest owned by the Forestry Commission. Follow the metalled path forward, and rising gradually, for 130 yards, and then turn left through wooden passway to a narrower, very inviting forest path. Eventually this arrives at next passway and beyond it go left and down, thus adhering to your former direction.

Continue forward, disregarding all crossing and side tracks. When a road appears ahead, carry on to reach it by P. F. sign. It is the A4, but our journey along it is minimal. Turn right along the verge for only 150 yards, then right again as if to Kiln Cottage, and as indicated by P.F. sign. To begin with this is a gravel drive edging the forest. Soon it passes a house and pond left with Knowl Hill seen across the pastures beyond. When drive ends, climb stile into meadowland.

Take care at this point. Disregard both stile immediately left and path going off to right, and continue forward through the long meadow. Path faint here, but it bears slightly right, more or less in line with right-hand hedge, to reach stile at far side by some sheep pens. Stile is marked by a green footpath sign, and beyond turn left for the few steps, and next stile ushers you to road.

Go right for 70 yards, then right once more on unmistakable P.F. leading back into forest. Soon twisting uphill, this path can be muddy in patches. Carry on, guided by W.A.s till just past a house, left, a crossing track is met. Turn left along it to very shortly face a house, The Warren, where go left down secluded by-road. When, at the bottom, road turns left go with it, disregarding bridleway through farm to right. You thus come up to meet a further road in which turn right.

Quite soon reach the one pub of the walk, The Red House at Warren Row, where take no heed of P.F. left, but a few steps further on do follow P.F. right. Again it is a gravel drive at first, but it is speedily replaced by a trim green path, garden left. Cross stile at end, to return to meadowland. The path tends to fade out here, so walk in accordance with right hedge —thus following meadow quite some distance round till you discover a waymarked stile in far corner. Climb, and a couple of steps on, go left along a single file track. In season delicate cow parsley decorates the banks in the most charming disarray.

Stay with this track for ¼ mile, and then watch out for a stile at top of right hand bank. It is indicated by a low stone plinth saying **Footpath to Honey Lane,** but these low signs tend to get overgrown.

Over stile Channers Wood is seen on the horizon away to right, and a fenced path takes you on and up field to cross stile at top, and a second ahead. You have arrived at a concrete drive; follow it forwards, ignoring turn right. Fields left, where sheep will most likely be grazing on the experimental seedings of the Grassland Research team.

On reaching wide farm track on right, turn along it as guided by W.A. on fence post, i.e. do not follow very narrow P.F. alongside. Stay with drive, which was also encountered on Walk 5, and, going through a gate on the way, arrive at Hall-place Farm. In farmyard turn right, then immediately left as signs show.

Leave farm and turn right up road. At the top see a post-box facing you at the T-junction, and cross to go past it and on P.F. going forward up into wood. Take no heed of any side-tracks, till you come to the metal path on which the walk began. By turning left along it you will regain the car park.

Refreshments: The Cafe, and The Crown, Burchetts Green. They face each other on the A404.—The Red House, Warren Row.

Wargrave

**Wargrave Hill, Highfield Farm, Crazies Hill,
Cockpole Green, Wargrave Manor.
5 miles.**

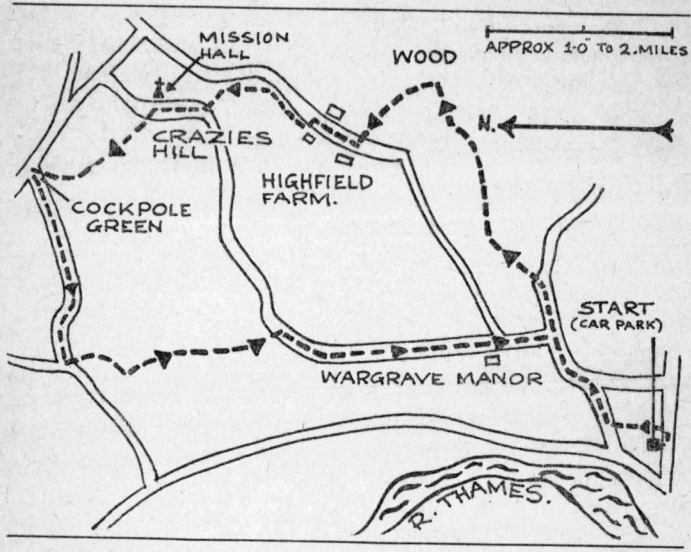

A very good walk, mainly on fieldpaths with a few short lengths along peaceful lanes. Several superb viewpoints dot the route, the variety of the terrain encourages a wide range of birds, and in the right season the keen-eyed will spot blackberries, elder, and cobnuts. Can be muddy here and there after heavy rain.

How to get there—By car to car park in School Lane, behind the Greyhound.

By train to Wargrave. Walk to centre of town, and just beyond traffic lights find the Greyhound.

By bus, Thames Valley 28/28a Reading-High Wycombe. Alight at the Greyhound.

From the car park turn left up School Lane, and almost at once left again up the no through road humorously named Backsideans. When it twists right leave it to go left by street lamp on pathway which hastily turns right to be walled on either side. On arrival at road turn right. You are now walking up Wargrave Hill, and when 10 ft. wall right ends, ignore P.F. right and carry on.

Keep ahead, disregarding all turnings off, till P.F. is reached on left.

Go through gate to follow well-used path bisecting field. At far side use gate, and keep ahead beside a grove of oak and sycamore. The next gate has a 3-armed P.F. sign beside it, but still go forward. One of the several streamlets watering these fields is to right, probably hidden by overgrowth in summer. When a gateway is reached, also right, go through or over stile alongside. Then sharp left along field till stile is met. Beyond it are several paths, but the way remains ahead along the bottom of a small, square meadow for about 50 yards, where climb stile left to enter wood.

Follow clear path up the gradual incline, being careful as it can be slippery if wet. Narrowing, it becomes more open and ultimately ends at a 4-armed sign, and an ideal spot at which to pause, look and listen.

On over stile and diagonally across field to far corner and exit to road by means of a stile to face an old grinding-stone in front of a farm outbuilding. Go right up road past Highfield Farm. Ignore first P.F. left, but 40 yards beyond it take next P.F., also left, through gate to walk on a raised bank parallel with road.

When it ends a further gate leads to field. Path may not be visible, but walk diagonally across field to discover a gate, arched by hazel, 50 yards from far left-hand corner. Beyond gate path continues between bracken and crosses a plank bridging streamlet into wood. Here go left, speedily over second streamlet, on, over stile, and up to P.F. sign and firm gravel track.

Turn left towards houses and road, then right up road, passing the Old Post House, to Crazies Hill.

Near the Mission Hall, which obligingly has a clock, ignore footpaths to left and right, but a yard or so on take next one on left. Reach stile into field, walk diagonally left, school seen to right, to gate taking you to cultivated land. Ahead beside tall thorn hedge right. Cross a somewhat awkward stile, and keep your direction till dense hedge ends. Here is a stile, climb, and go diagonally over grass to far corner and stile to road; this is Cockpole Green.

Immediately go left down single track road cutting between fields, where, forever foraging, seagulls follow the farmer. Stay with road, eventually winding downhill to a junction. Abandon road here to go left via gate into a rising meadow.

Bear left, abiding by line of left hedgerow, to gain top of rise where trees and wire fence stop. Underfoot the path may now have vanished, but the way is straight on downhill. Look out for stile by gate in bottom hedge, climb to a crossing track, turn right a couple of strides, then left over next stile.

Walk forward up left edge of meadow towards a fine beech hanger. At top cross stile, and still on and up. If the path is overgrown here and there it is of short duration, and a stile on left returns you to grassland. Continue with hedge to right till a stile acts as exit to road.

Turn right along road, for ¾ mile, passing Manor Farm and the grounds of Wargrave Manor, and ignoring turning left to Warren Row. On arrival at T-junction, which you will recognise, simply go right to retrace your steps back to Wargrave.

Refreshments   Several inns in Wargrave.

Wargrave

**School Hill, Ruscombe, Hare Hatch,
Bear Grove, Blakes Lane.
6½ miles.**

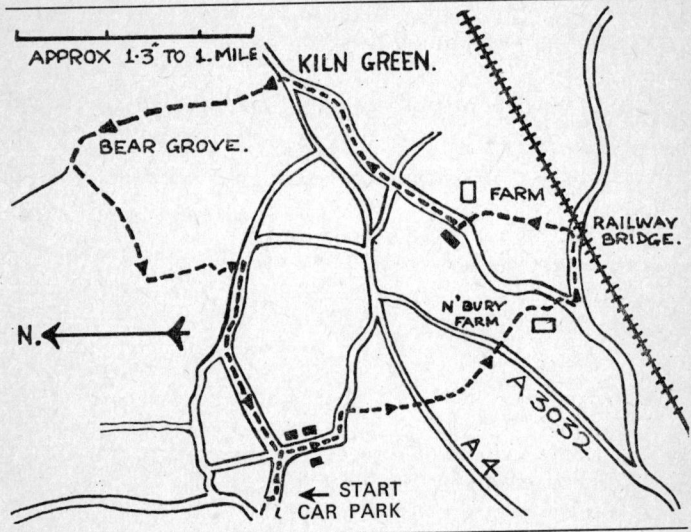

This is a fairly strenuous route which is recommended as a bracing and pleasing form of exercise in the late autumn, or winter, when there is a decided nip in the air. Perfect for working up a good appetite for lunch or dinner. The paths continue without let or hindrance, the stretches of lane nearly all have verges, and there are one or two panoramic views. After heavy rain, do be prepared for some mud.

How to get there—As Walk 7.

Come out of the car park in School Lane and turn left up the road, i.e. away from the Greyhound. At top bear right up School Hill to pass Piggott Junior School. When houses are left behind ignore footpath to right, and carry on to a bridleway also right, and near a Mumbury Hill sign. Leave road to follow the broad way, with extensive views all around. Pass a private path to right, and when field ends carry on forward to road. Cross, to walk along bridleway opposite, soon bordered left by a row of spindly conifers. They cease at a gathering of tracks, when go half-left on broad open track to road.

Cross, and again ahead on clear way, thicket hedge right. When gravel drive develops go with it, winding away from the twin-gabled Northbury Farm, to a further road. Turn right for 50 yards to road junction, and then left as to Windsor, with the square tower of Ruscombe Church away to right.

After a good $\frac{1}{4}$ mile, and just prior to railway bridge, go left on bridleway. When it divides, near farm, take left fork to arrive at road. Go right along road, soon passing a Hare Hatch sign, till you meet a road junction. Go over and along lane as signposted to Knowl Hill. Ignore footpaths by Scarletts Farm, and carry on till main road is reached.

Here, cross with appropriate care, and go up No Through Road passing the St. John's Convent for retired priests on left. As road (it is Bear Hill Road, but there is nothing to tell you so) comes to a full stop, a cart track leads you on and through the woodland of Bear Grove. Stay with this attractive shaded track, gradually moving uphill. After about 1 mile find track joining from right by a 3-armed signpost. Walk ahead a yard or two to further sign, and take left cart track downhill. Ignore a further sign passed after about 100 yards. Proceed ahead for further 200 yards and at a timber felling area left, turn right on Public Footpath and over stile.

Walk on to soon leave wood by next stile, and be greeted by the enchantment of a distant pastoral view. Narrowing, the path goes slowly downhill, passes briefly through a patch of wooded land, and emerges over a stile into a charming little square meadow (if you have followed Walk 7 you will recognise it). Follow meadowpath ahead up over the slight rise, and at far side you will come upon a signpost.

Turn left on well-trodden path, houses of Wargrave glimpsed briefly to right. Descending slowly, eventually meet a gravel track, where merely walk forward to road. Turn right along it, Blakes Lane, till you reach Victoria Road, which will lead you back to School Lane.

Refreshments   As Walk 7.

Pangbourne

Shooters Hill, Pangbourne Nautical College, Tidmarsh, River Pang.
5 miles.

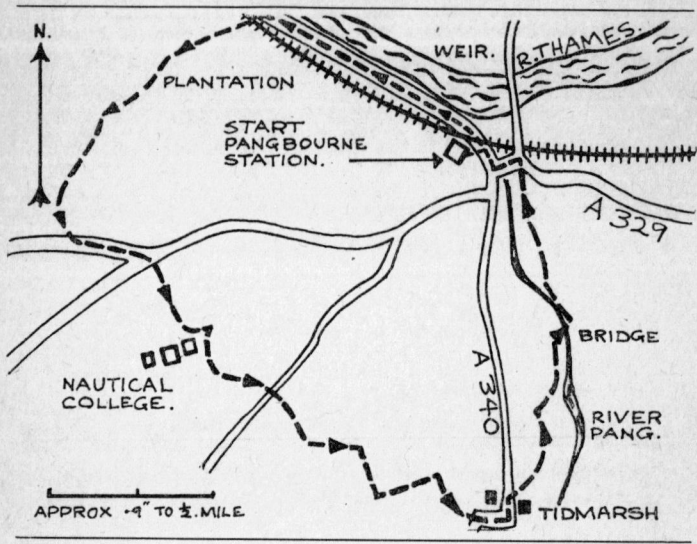

Pangbourne is a first class base from which to explore the well-wooded and unspoilt surrounding countryside. Try this route in spring, when the winter branches are just tipped with green, and the birds, more easily seen before the full foliage appears, are in good voice! The modest River Pang, met on return, is a clear, sparkling stream.

How to get there—By car to car park on corner of Station Road and St. James' Close, the town side of station.

By train to Pangbourne.

By bus: Alder Valley No. 5 Reading-Oxford. Alight in Station Road.

Fortunately car park, bus stop and station all lie within a

few yards of each other, so whatever your mode of transport the starting point is more or less the same.

From the car park turn left to go under railway bridge, and along road to pass station entrance left and the Swan and spectacular weir right. It is a spot well known to readers of Jerome K. Jerome, for here his three men gave up their boat in favour of the train which took them back to town.

Continue beside river. One group of the extravagant houses you pass is known locally as 'The Seven Deadly Sins'.

When, after approximately ½ mile, the houses end, soon come to a parking space on the river bank facing a sign, Shooters Hill. Here turn left and under the railway arch to immediately see a P.F. bearing left; then forward again.

As it moves hastily on through a young forestry plantation this path is considerably more inviting than it appears at first. Soon cross low stile, and ahead, climbing almost imperceptibly out of the valley. When you reach stage where fields are directly to left, follow path swinging right, and, once over next stile, enter a beechwood. Keep to forward track, cutting its way amidst an unusual spread of bramble undergrowth till you emerge by a kissing-gate into meadowland.

Straight ahead by hedged fence, and as it ends at a kissing-gate to wide drive, ignore, and bear diagonally right over field to another kissing-gate in far corner. Go through to pass a gate, cross stile and carry on beside left edge of field to road and P.F. sign. Take due care on stepping out to road because any passing motorist will have little warning of your arrival. Then turn left along road passing buildings of Pangbourne College, the training school for both the Services and the Merchant Navy. Disregard drive left and lane right after 150 yards, and keep on for further 100 yards to road junction. Cross road to walk on up Private Road opposite.

Don't be diverted by any side tracks, but stay with road till a crossing road is met, just short of low college buildings. Turn left, and when buildings cease turn right to gain a gravel track. Follow it, to briefly have brick wall right; and beyond a house, Riverdell, bear left with track. On meeting narrow by-road, simply cross to go straight forward on firm, dry track soon bounded by mixed hedgerows. After some distance, and beyond a solitary house right, follow the track as it dwindles to a narrow pathway. Soon it bears left and onwards with a luxuriant growth of hedge dividing you from the extensive farmland on either side. If the shrubs prove to be mildly obstructive here and there, it is easy to find a way round, and there is a clear length of path awaiting you. Eventually, note a twin telegraph pole—the path has kept in line with the poles —and go directly right down field by distinct path. Hedge to left only now.

Soon pass a post bearing a rough sign 'PUBL. FOOTPATH', and continue forward, then left and later right on well-defined grassed track. When a gate is reached go through and over field to use kissing-gate to road and P.F. sign. Walk left for 100 yards to face the Greyhound at Tidmarsh, cross road and turn left as signposted to Pangbourne.

Directions which follow are also applicable to the end of Walk 11.

About 100 yards on, past house, Sunnybrook, turn right via kissing-gate into meadow. Follow path travelling left to edge the end of gardens, and soon go over stile situated very close to hedge. Walk on to use next stile by chestnut paling fence, and still forward. Stay with path passing houses, till the Old Rectory Cottage is passed right. Here, go a step or two forward towards white gate to find a stile by another gate on your right. Climb, and simply go diagonally across grass to stile in left-hand corner.

Now the little River Pang appears, and the way continues along the river bank till a bridge is reached. Walk over bridge to a 3-armed P.F. sign and then turn left on clear path following opposite river bank till you meet a metal gate at far side of meadow. Go through, and along forward path.

The houses of Pangbourne come into view, and when at length a P.F. sign is passed carry on ahead on un-made road. It is The Moors as you will discover at its other end where it meets the town. Here turn left back to the station and car park.

Pangbourne

**Pangbourne Meadow, Mapledurham Lock,
Purley.
5½ miles.**

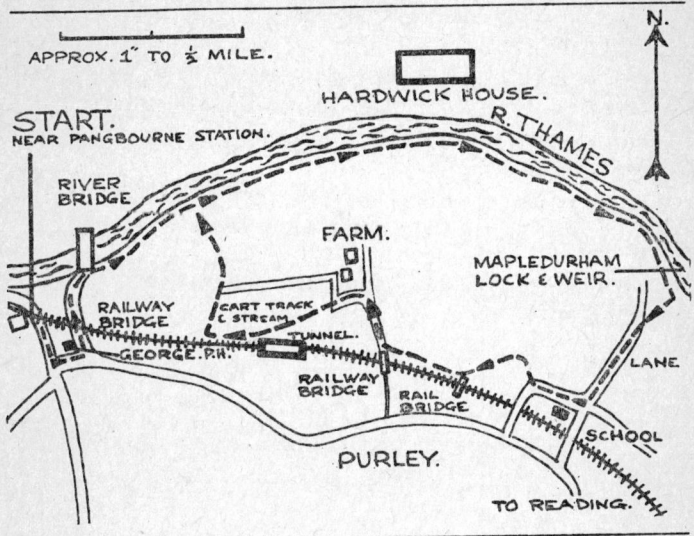

Perfect for a summer's day. The paths are level. There is water to cool your feet and hands if need be, and all the life of the lovely reach of the Thames to entertain you. This is the riverside of Kenneth Grahame, and the incomparable Toad, Mole and 'dear good old Ratty', who 'sometimes wandered countrywards, crossed a field or two of pasturage'. Which is exactly what this route does before coming full circle back to the river again.

How to get there—As Walk 9.

On coming out of car park go down High Street as signposted to Reading, and turn left by the George on the Whitchurch road. Go under the railway bridge, and follow road till you have passed a Berkshire County sign just short of the bridge. Here follow path right, and parallel with road, to cross stile and reach the river bank.

Turn right along the towpath; this is Pangbourne Meadow, 7 acres of National Trust land. Merely continue beside the river and on seeing a 3-armed P.F. sign still go on. Soon Hardwick House, with its gables and mullioned windows, is seen across the water, and finally, after 2 miles, you will arrive at Mapledurham Lock.

Go through the gate, past the lock-keeper's house and, after a natural pause to admire his prize-winning garden, and, of course, to enjoy the spectacle of the weir, it is here that the route departs from the river.

Leave lock by a second gate and follow P.F. going right over the grass to reach a lane. Forward along it, past gate and ahead till a road is met. Turn right along road, and on through the village, passing Purley Village School to left. When road bends left, desert it to turn sharp right on public bridleway— sign may be partially obscured. Follow round curve of left-hand wall, and then go with path as, narrowing, it winds right and is now hedged left.

On arrival at railway bridge do not be diverted, but walk ahead, wire fence left, and a generous sweep of the Chiltern escarpment filling the far horizon. At next bridge turn right down road for about 300 yards. Then make a left turn, **not** over the cattle grid to the brick and timbered Scarces Farm, but along the lane. However, when it speedily bears right, leave it to go forward over stile on P.F. edging farmland. Once beyond next stile, continue to keep hard by left boundary of field. When a railway tunnel is reached, maintain your direction. Not very well defined here, the path continues ahead with wire fencing dividing it from the railway bank left.

After passing a pylon arrive at a cart track, and turn right along it. You are now beside a half-hidden stream which broadens and becomes increasingly attractive as you follow its course all the way down to the Thames. Now you will see a 3-armed P.F. sign which you will recognise. Turn left to retrace your steps along the towpath back to Pangbourne.

Pangbourne

**Sulham Woods, Long Lane,
Tidmarsh, River Pang.
5½ miles.**

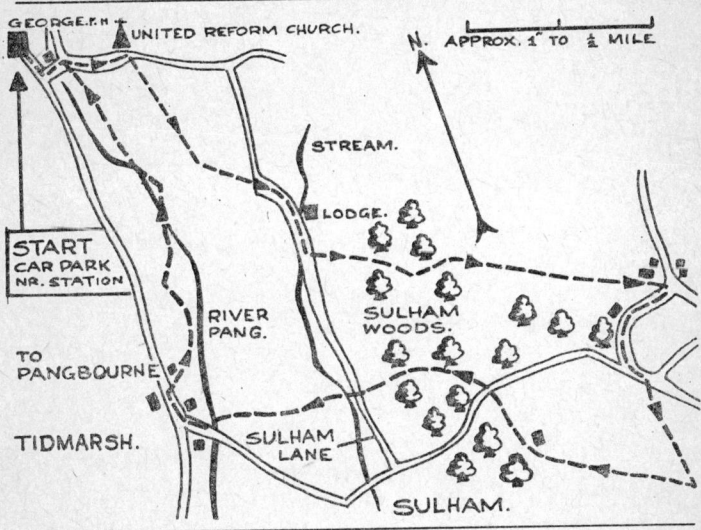

Making use of quiet paths and lanes south of the town, this is an attractive and peaceful route wandering in and out of Sulham Woods, which is Forestry Commission land. It returns via Tidmarsh, and for the last mile only, follows the same route at walk 9.

How to get there—As Walk 9.

Leave the car park and go up the High Street, pass the George and continue up the Reading Road till the United Reform Church is passed left. A few yards beyond turn right up signposted P.F. On meeting road, cross, and continue on P.F. opposite to next road. Go forward over it and ahead on path running between allotments, and leaving the town behind you use kissing-gate at end, by a 4-armed signpost, and walk straight on over gorse-studded meadow, ignoring side paths, to cross a white railed footbridge.

Still ahead, and at far side of this field a stile ushers you into Sulham Lane. Turn right for 200 yards where lane bridges a stream, and a lodge is to left. Now keep on for further 150 yards and then cross stile in hedge to left, which is easily missed if you don't keep a sharp look out for it.

Walk straight up field and at top enter the Forestry Commission's Sulham Woods. Follow the track before you, briefly very steep, and disregarding all tracks and turnings off, keep directly on through the wood as the beech are supplanted by conifers. At far boundary climb stile and walk on path across open farmland ringed by trees. The unmistakable way soon winds round some bushes and proceeds up the gentle rise of next field. Soon spy a lonely stile ahead, and beyond it walk towards a group of houses.

On reaching a low stile on left, cross and forward along path to driveway taking you to road facing Dark Lane. Turn right along Long Lane, away from houses. Pass Cartwheel Cottage, right, and carry on along lane to road junction. Go over, to climb stile, slightly left, and follow narrow path over field. When woodland bounds your left hand, go on up till it ceases at a double P.F. sign.

Turn very sharp right on well defined path; this is the turning back point. Eventually see pond right and the barely recognisable site of the vanished Sulham Farm. A few steps on your track ends, and a further Forestry plantation is seen left. But our way is right on cart track travelling, past another pond, to lane. Cross and re-enter Sulham Woods.

(The next short stretch, though visually a rather lovely way, tends in part to be exceptionally muddy after rain. So if you need an alternative route, just turn left and follow road for about a mile till you reach the Greyhound at Tidmarsh. Then return to Pangbourne as detailed in Walk 9.)

Of the pair of tracks facing you, use the left-hand, through a young plantation including oak, willow, birch and fir. Disregard tracks off till you soon arrive at a small triangular clearing. Identify it by a gorse bush towards the right-hand corner and a line of oaks in front of you. Again follow the left-hand fork, oaks passed to right, winding downhill to leave wood by a small gate.

Carry straight on down left edge of field. At bottom bear right for a step or so to come out in Sulham Lane. Now go left for another few steps, right over stile and forward over meadow to cross stream by a footbridge. Carry on ahead along right edge of field, with occasional white railings on right, till a stone footbridge is reached. Cross, and with hedge left, ahead to stile giving on to driveway and stream, where stepping a few paces left brings you to road.

Turn right along road to quickly reach Tidmarsh and the Greyhound, where bear right as signposted to Pangbourne.

From here the return to Pangbourne follows the route detailed from the Greyhound in Walk 9.

Refreshments The Pantry, Pangbourne. Greyhound, Tidmarsh, and inns in Pangbourne.

Bucklebury Common

Turners Green, The Slade,
Upper Common, Hopwoods Green.
5 miles.

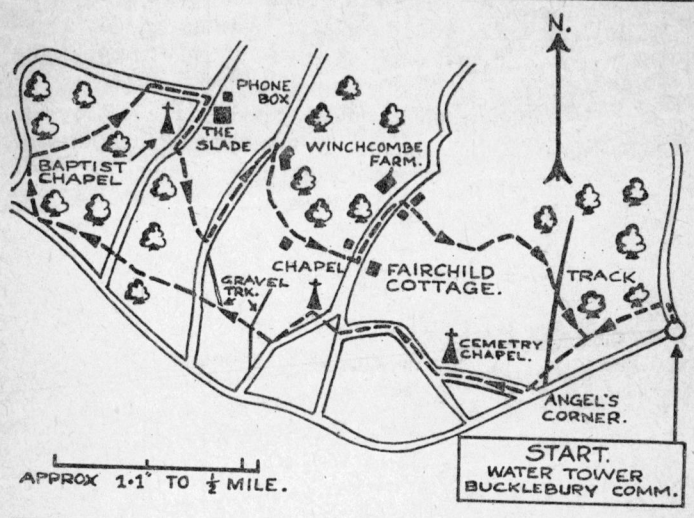

Bucklebury Common, 5 miles east of Newbury, just north of the A4, is criss-crossed by both paths and minor roads. There are said to be nearly 300 footpaths in the 5 mile length of the Common! Because of this, and the fact that there are very few signposts, extra care is advised in following the directions. Clothed by a wealth of wild flowers, bracken, bramble, and other shrubs and trees, this is splendid walking country, the footpaths being well trodden and in good order.

How to get there—By car, to a car park on the road from Chapel Row to Upper Bucklebury (it has several parking areas) by the Bucklebury Common Water Tower at the crossroads 1 mile west of Chapel Row.

By bus: Alder Valley No. 11/11a Newbury-Oxford and alight at the Water Tower.

Begin by going down road to Bucklebury Village for only 50 yards, where turn left on bridleway. Surfaced initially, it crosses the Common, and on it forking, keep ahead. Disregard all side tracks and reach road at Angel's Corner, by a Scout Camp Site. Go right, that is on the quiet minor road branching off from main road, to shortly pass a pair of houses. On passing the Cemetery Chapel right, meet further road and turn right along it.

Follow it round and down to pass several very attractive thatched cottages, and then up out of dip to a crossroads. Straight across, and on to next crossing road, and again ahead on No Through Road to Turners Green. But only as far as the Chapel and Appletree Cottage, opposite, where turn sharp left on a clear, unmarked track over the Common. On meeting road merely walk a couple of steps right to see track obviously continuing, now through woodland.

A few yards on several paths converge, so stay on right fork to emerge on open ground again. When it is crossed by a gravel track, continue ahead, but when it forks use left fork to reach road. Cross, follow narrower, shaded path forward to next road. Over, and along path opposite. Don't worry when it splits, either hand will do as, like many of the Common tracks, they rejoin shortly.

Another road is met which ignore, and bear sharp right along wide track. On arrival at a crossing track, just short of next road, do not go forward to road, instead turn right along the track, and at a clearing, identified by its group of mature beech, use either fork. Eventually re-emerge on the open Common, where, at a crossing track, carry on forward. Houses are glimpsed right, and when track develops into a broad clearing, with a track crossing it and red brick house right, the way is still ahead to road.

A right turn now, downhill, using visible telephone kiosk as a landmark. On arrival at road junction turn right along road. You have arrived at The Slade. Abide by road, passing the post-box, and immediately beyond the Baptist Chapel, and opposite Slade Cottage, turn directly left. Again there is no sign, but the footway over the grass is perfectly distinct as it sets off over the Upper Common. Ignore stile seen left after a few yards, and keep with path moving right. But when it splits follow left and lower fork to walk over the tiniest of bridges. Slightly uphill here, and on leaving wood behind take forward left fork, still up.

Now, when next road is encountered, do **not** use path facing you; instead turn left along road for $\frac{1}{2}$ mile almost to Hopwoods Green. Directly prior to a Z bend road sign and Hopwoods Green sign, turn right on wide gravel track. At first it is also a driveway to a group of bungalows, so simply follow it round as it curves right, and at some stabling left take left fork, staying with it going down and up again under the trees. When your path is crossed by another, wooden gate and solitary Dutch barn left, maintain your direction, in spite of inviting green ride right.

The woodland path you are treading finally ends at a road opposite Fairchild Cottage; only its chimneys are spied above the high hedge. Go left, past house called Briff, for 300 yards, where, at Winchcombe Farm, turn right down No Through Road. Once beyond the last house, the road peters out to a rough track. Follow it upwards to enter the wood, and on path dividing, use right and forward fork, still up. When you meet a crossing track, cottage right, bear right for 12 paces, and then follow left fork.

Ignore all paths branching off, and carry on till, just prior to road, a wide crossing track is met. Turn left along it for 300 yards back to road. A few yards right again returns you to the Water Tower.

Refreshments   This is excellent picnic country. Singing Kettle, Stanford Dingley. The Bull, Stanford Dingley.

Bucklebury Common

Lower Common, Redhill Copse, Bucklebury, Pangfield Farm, Chapel Row.
7 miles.

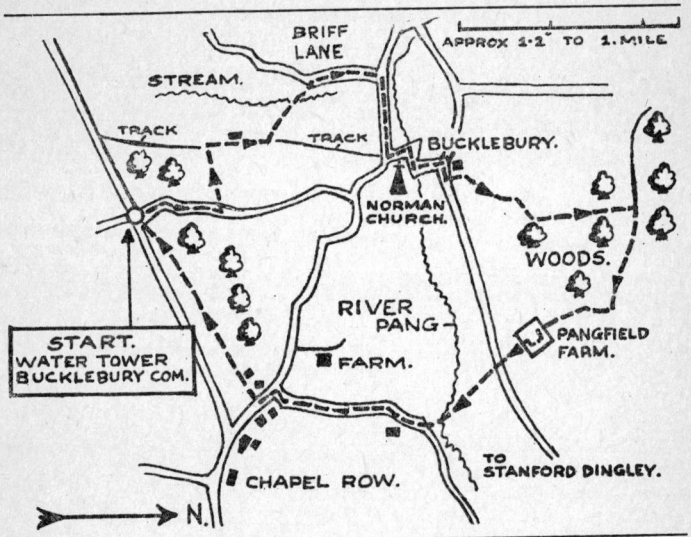

Beginning like Walk 12 from the Water Tower on Bucklebury Common, this longer, more adventurous route delving into remote country, enjoys the more varied interest of common, wooded and farming land, and has the added bonus of extensive views. It does, however, include one brief stretch requiring a certain amount of agility, and it can be muddy in places.

How to get there—As Walk 12.

Alternative parking in Bucklebury Village near church and pick up walk from (A).

From the Water Tower go down road signposted to Bucklebury village, and at the double bridleway sign turn right for only a couple of steps, then left beneath a twin-trunked oak.

The track, on the Lower Common, runs more or less parallel with the road, passes a group of spectacular redwoods, and after ¼ mile re-meets road. Go right along it for 200 yards, and a few yards short of a pair of attractive gabled cottages turn left along an obvious path. A gap in the hedge on the corner frames an unexpectedly lovely pastoral view.

Travelling down, then gradually up again this shady path leaves the trees at a crossing track, where go forward left, and 100 yards along meet a second crossing track. Sharp right here on most inviting open track, bounded by hedgerows. Beyond a house, Vanners, the track, continuing forward, narrows to become deeply shaded, and soon divides. Follow left fork to an antiquated stile into meadow.

Continue in line with right edge of meadow. Towards far side, aim at left-hand corner to discover—you will probably need to search for it—a gap in hedgerow where narrow path goes through the undergrowth, and abruptly **down. Watch your step here.** There is a stream to be crossed, it's only a stride wide, and then climb up steep ascent of opposite bank. It can be extremely slippery, and I needed a helping hand!

Once at the top, go right to enter Redhill Copse. This is Forestry Commission territory, and especially after rain the air is sweet with the mingled scent of pines, honeysuckle and the carefully preserved wayside flowers. The F.C. path brings you to a road, Briff Lane, in which turn right for ¼ mile to road junction. Go right as sign-posted to Bucklebury; the church tower soon hoves into view. At next junction, just before the church (of Norman origin with an elaborately carved doorway leading to an interesting interior) turn left.

(A) Follow road towards Stanford Dingley, pass post office, over bridge crossing the River Pang, and on to meet next junction where go right as to Stanford Dingley for only 80 yards, and see a No Through Road, to Hawkridge House, on left.

Here you have a choice. If some rather rugged walking does **not** appeal to you then the easier way is keep with road for the best part of a mile to rejoin the main route at the entrance to drive up to Pangfield Farm, which is clearly marked .(Now as from (B)).

Otherwise, be prepared for slightly heavier going in truly rural surroundings and a path, approaching Pangfield Farm, which tends to get overgrown, though not impassably.

For the main route turn left up the No Through Road. Near top of this unspoilt lane pass an admirable brick and timber house left, and bear round to right as if approaching next house. Walk a short way up, and then, short of the garden, branch left on path which, a few steps on, meets a footpath sign. Careful here. Do not continue round to left as the sign suggests, but stay with your path, veering right and upwards, house right, being screened by shrubs. Once house is behind you, the path is unmistakable with wire fence left, separating you from a young plantation, and woodland right.

The next landmark is a spacious crossing track which disregard, and carry on ahead up into wood till you come out at the summit. Turn right on a grass ride, equalling the ancient Ridgeway path in its broad expanse. Shortly there are banks of rhododendrons left, and a little further on the way is downhill and the ride ends at a hedge. Admittedly the path is well secreted here, but by turning sharp right away from the ride you will find a path of single file width—like going from the sublime to the ridiculous—cutting through the entanglement of lush grass and bracken.

This continues on the edge of woodland, and as it leaves wood to continue ahead as a densely shaded way between fields, keep your direction till you arrive at Pangfield Farm and see a couple of white footpath signs. One points the way you have walked, and the other directs you left for 20 yards, where see a notice guiding you round back of farm, and finally left down farm drive. The path has been diverted to skirt, rather than run straight through the farm.

(B) The drive delivers you to road, by Pangfield Farm sign, where alternative route rejoins. Cross road, over stile opposite, and green path leads ahead, over another stile, and curves slightly right across next field. At far side a sign guides you to go left via gate and by right edge of field to its far right-hand corner. At this stage cross stream, it is the little River Pang again, by a make-shift bridge with hand rails, and go straight up field, through gate to road.

Walk right up road past Bucklebury Lodge to make a steady climb of about ¾ mile to where road from Bucklebury village merges from right. Continue left and forward for 100 yards only. Then, using Chapel Row Farm as a distinctive landmark, turn right on an unmarked track wandering off over Lower Common.

Innumerable tracks have been trodden out hereabouts. But if, by avoiding all tracks off, you keep to the directions, you will regain the Water Tower.

On the track from road being replaced by gravel, it veers left to a T-junction. Turn right for a step or so, then left to pass several individual houses right. At meeting of several tracks, go forward, and on your track splitting keep to left fork. At next meeting of tracks, still forward maintaining a west-south-west direction. At next crossing track, by Barber's Pightel, follow left track winding round and disregarding all diversions till you reach road. Here turn right back to Water Tower.

Refreshments   Singing Kettle, Stanford Dingley. The Bull, Stanford Dingley. Ice-cream at Village Store, Bucklebury.

Bucklebury Common

**Lower Common, Midgham,
Midgham Park, Carbins Wood.
3½ miles.**

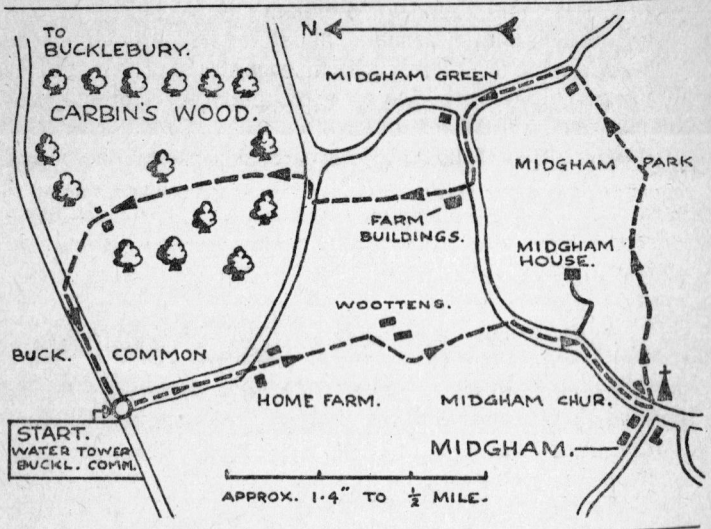

This short route, taking in some fine parkland and a brief stretch of Forestry land, is certain to be found enjoyable at all times. On the way you will meet rather more gates than stiles, so do please remember the Countryside Code and make sure all gates are closed firmly behind you.

How to get there—As Walk 12.

Once again, like Walks 12 and 13, this one sets off from the Water Tower at the crossroads 1 mile west of Chapel Row.

Leaving the Tower cross over to go down road signposte to Midgham for about ¼ mile, where note bridleways on eith side. By-pass these, but 40 yards on, when road bends le leave it to go ahead on gravel track passing Home Farm rig

Carry on along track till you meet gateway to house called Woottens. Here go slightly right, and through gate marked 'Footpath'.

The path skirts the lovely, mellow house, and goes over stile into meadow, where the spire of Midgham church is seen thrusting up above the distant trees. Walk forward to visible gate leading to lane. Turn right along the quiet lane, staying with it as it winds round to Midgham church. Here, the way is not through church grounds, but sharp left through a wide gate with lodge left. This path is unsignposted, but just carry on as gravel drive gives way to grass, and you are quickly led, via next gate, into Midgham Park.

In the parkland follow obvious path, as it passes a holly tree left, and wends its way down beneath an avenue of oaks. At bottom of dip walk through gate, and ahead as path, now fenced on either side, takes you on through further gate. When, almost at once, path divides, keep to left fork which brings you to a gravel drive.

Cross, through opposite gate, and still ahead up parkland, grounds of Midgham House left, to cross stile within sight of a summerhouse and private lake. Then carry on ahead—though it is worth looking back for the view—following the slightly sunken track, bearing a little left.

On it rising out of the hollow, a white lodge is spied ahead. Negotiate next stile-cum-gate, and walk on to reach lodge. Having undone the tall metal gate, and, of course, secured it again, you will find yourself in road, where turn left.

After about ¼ mile arrive at a junction, where cottage at Midgham Green seen off to right has diminutive dormers in its thatch. Oddly enough our route is not as directed to Bucklebury, but left towards Midgham. Stay with this road, winding uphill, for only 250 yards, and then turn right along road passing farm buildings left. At next junction turn right for about 50 paces. Keep a sharp eye open here for stile on left; it is set well back from road behind a holly bush.

Beyond stile walk by left edge of meadow. At far side maintain direction along next one, as path leads you on and down to enter Carbins Wood (Forestry Commission) by a wooden wicket gate. In wood follow narrow path twisting between the

48

trees, somewhat muddily for a brief patch, but speedily developing into a broad green ride. Ignore all side tracks, and carry on to eventually reach a Forestry Commission board, and stile, which climb.

Ahead, on clear path, dipping down and up again to emerge at gravel track by King Charles' Cottage.

After a few steps forward there is a crossing track which ignore, and keep on along wide track cutting through Bucklebury Common to end at the road. Then by turning left for about 300 yards you will regain the Water Tower.

Refreshments Singing Kettle, Stanford Dingley. The Bull, Stanford Dingley.

West Ilsley

**Ridgeway Path, Bury Down,
Sheep Down (North-west of W. Ilsley).
4½ miles.**

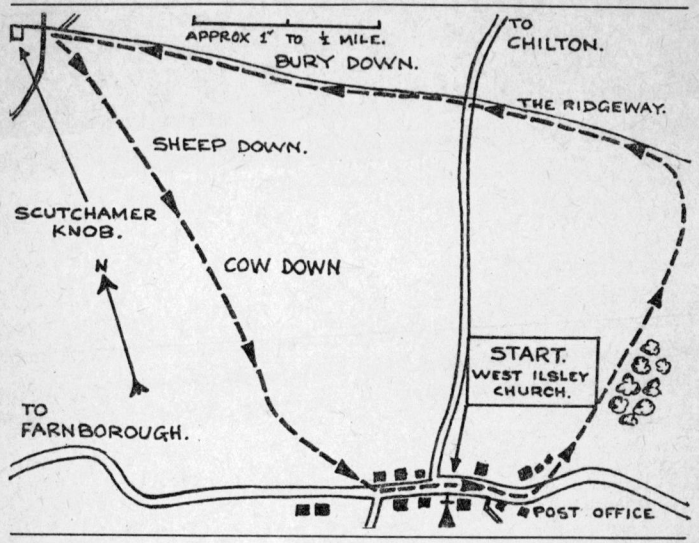

Setting off from the secluded village of West Ilsley this is a downland walk, on which to enjoy a fine selection of chalk-loving flowers, long, unobstructed views, and the rolling pattern of the Berkshire downs.

It incorporates, as do Walks 16 and 17, a short section of the Ridgeway Long-Distance path which travels 85 miles from Avebury in Wiltshire to Ivinghoe in Buckinghamshire, **the** highway of the downs. (See 'Walks along the Ridgeway', Spurbooks).

Walking on the downs is exhilarating whatever the time of year, but it can be very cold in winter, so be prepared. On the other hand, if warm, there is often a welcome and refreshing breeze.

How to get there—By car to West Ilsley and park in the village. Alternative parking at top of Bury Down, 1 mile north of village, where the Ridgeway Path crosses the road, and pick up walk at (A). This will shorten the walk by about $1\frac{1}{2}$ miles.

Facing West Ilsley Church turn left to walk through village. More or less as it ends, just past Post Office right, and The Malt House left, turn left up a sign-posted cart track. When, beyond a handful of cottages, the track divides follow right fork uphill.

Notice how a varied bushrow shelters your right hand, while the other less interesting thorn hedge is not high enough to screen the view.

Keep with track. After about 1 mile it curves gently left, and the smoking towers of Harwell—they do make a good landmark—are seen ahead. But a short distance on reach the Ridgeway.

Though not signposted here, the spacious green track trodden out by pre-historic man, his sheep and his cattle, and still virtually unchanged, is over 30 yards wide in places, and unmistakable. Turn left along it journeying over Bury Down till, about $\frac{1}{2}$ mile on, you reach a road and one of the oak signposts put up by the Countryside Commission to mark the course of the Ridgeway.

(A) Cross road, and carry on along the Ridgeway (with the Harwell Atomic Energy Research Establishment below right) which rises almost imperceptibly towards a distant plantation.

There are numerous Gallops hereabouts, for this is horse-training country; one runs left of this stretch of the Ridgeway. Walkers are courteously asked to abide by the path.

Continue for about 1 mile, that is until you are some $\frac{1}{4}$ mile short of the obvious plantation (near Scutchamer Knob) ahead. Now look for two paths joining the Ridgeway from the right, within a few yards of each other. Use as landmarks only, and turn left. Once across the Gallop, turn left again so that, with the plantation now behind you, you are facing the direction from which you've come.

Walk forward a few yards, with another Gallop off to your right, to reach a small arable field. From here a clearer path develops, curving away right, and soon moving slowly downhill in a S.S.E. direction, parallel with Gallop. Follow the path as it leads down Sheep Down.

Not long after the buildings of West Ilsley appear in the valley below, pass a small sign 'Please keep to the footpath'. Without further ado the path swings rather more sharply downwards to join a wider, hedged track. This takes you to the road and a bridleway sign in West Ilsley. Turn left past The Harrow and back to regain church.

Refreshments   The Harrow, West Ilsley en route.

East Ilsley

**Ridgeway, Sheep Down (North-east of W. Ilsley),
Gore Hill, Hodcott Down, Yewtree Hill.
5 miles.**

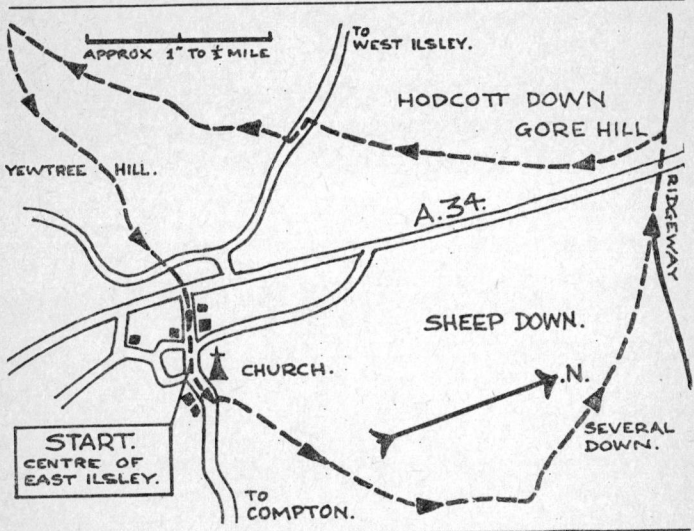

East Ilsley, with its decorative pond, is one of the most charming of Berkshire villages. Lying in a remote dip in the downs, with the 13th century church standing apart on its own individual hillock, it is famed as a centre of race-horse training. The walker is frequently accompanied by the stirring sight of a string of horses being exercised. This downland route also follows the Ridgeway for part of the way, and indeed all that was said about Walk 15 is equally applicable here. The broad tracks, many of them bridleways, are perpetually inviting.

How to get there—By car to East Ilsley, and park in the village. Alternative parking can be found at the top of Gore Hill, where the Ridgeway Path, indicated by a low sign, crosses the A34; then pick up walk at (A).

From the Crown and Horns in the centre of East Ilsley go along road as to Compton passing pond, and probably a collection of duck, to right. When houses left cease, go left up marked bridleway. Keep ahead to soon pass notice asking you to abide by Right of Way. Thus, as you continue, a green Gallop is on your left.

The undeviating bridleway takes you to the top of the rise, and a further bridleway sign. Here turn left and after about 70 yards ignore a similar sign and carry straight ahead, Gallop still away to left. You have now joined the Ridgeway journeying over Sheep Down.

Look out for hares streaking over fields to right. Ignore all side tracks, and once past a Ridgeway signpost you may see an inconspicuous plaque to right. It commemorates a young 2nd Lieutenant in the Life Guards who lost his life in an accident while on Military duty in 1947.

Shortly, on arrival at road (A34) cross to regain the Ridgeway on opposite side.

(A) This is Gore Hill, and there is a low Ridgeway sign a few yards in from the road. Continue past it for only about 100 yards, then bear left on clear green path. Follow it, winding round the field, till it settles to a straightforward downhill track on the edge of Hodcott Down, and parallel with road.

Part way down, as path direction moves away from road, East Ilsley is distinctly seen, but its secluded position is quickly emphasised as, a short way on, it disappears behind the intervening hill. When, towards the bottom, the track forks keep to left fork to gain road.

At this point the walk may be curtailed by turning left along road, up the hill, and down to follow round under the tunnel into E. Ilsley. This will cut about 1 mile off the walk.

The more hardy, wishing to complete the longer route, should also go left up road, but only for 50 yards. Then right over stile by gate, and across field, bushes right, to next visible gate. Beyond it keep your direction by following right edge of very long field to its furthest corner and find a narrow lane, in which turn sharp left.

At first it is somewhat overgrown, but soon becomes clearer and more open. Stay with it as, rising slowly, it develops into a green path following right edge of field. It breasts the rise of Yewtree Hill and takes you all the way back to East Ilsley.

Refreshments   Inns in East Ilsley.

Compton

**Roden Downs, Ridgeway, Compton Downs.
4½ miles.**

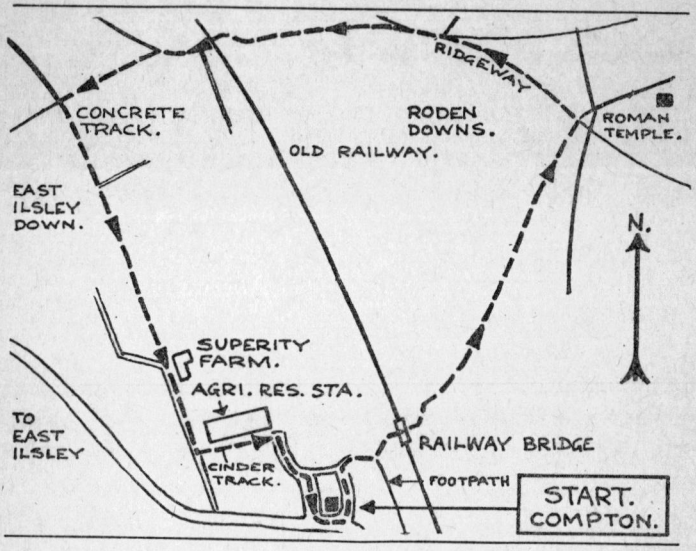

The third of these downland walks begins from the rather
larger village of Compton and goes up to the delightful Roden
Downs, where a little oasis of trees and shrubs makes it a
popular picnic place in summer. Walking these broad and
ancient tracks has a restorative quality, difficult to analyse, but
to which the late S. P. B. Mais paid tribute:– *'There is no
way I know of regaining happiness more surely than of
wandering along the Berkshire Downs.'*

How to get there—By car to Compton and park in village.

From the Swan in village turn up Horn Street which runs
alongside the inn. At top meet Wallingford Road and bear
right. Quickly by-pass footpaths right and follow road wind-

ing left to bring you to a railway bridge. Go under, then bear left, and after 60 yards, right, to go slowly uphill.

The firm track is shielded by tall hedgerows, which cease only as the open downland is reached. When the stony track swings left, just keep forward on green, rutted path till you arrive at a meeting of paths, and the attractive planting of trees and shrubs at the top of Roden Downs.

A short diversion here will take you, by going ahead and slightly right, to the site of the Roman Temple.

Our route turns sharp left to follow a section of the Ridgeway. When another track joins from right, go on, slightly downhill now, on a sunken chalk track. On it dividing, follow left fork, that is not towards farm buildings. One of the present joys of the Ridgeway is that it leads you purposefully on, with little diversion or need for direction.

So stay with it, dipping down and up again, over a disused railway, and on seeing a broad track left, still keep ahead.

As the path rises steadily, not even the distant smoke of Harwell can mar the pervading tranquility.

On eventual arrival at a concrete track, turn left along it, thus parting company with the Ridgeway which journeys north-west. Follow concrete track, and do not be surprised if a tractor or two come trundling by. Away to the right is East Ilsley, tucked neatly into a pocket of the downs.

When, just past Superity Farm, the track becomes a road, houses left, stay with it until a footpath sign is seen on right. Here, turn left along a cinder track beside the Isolation Compound of the Agricultural Research Council. The track ends at a road, where turn right down to Compton.

Refreshments   Inns in Compton village.

Hungerford

**Through farmland and open country to
Standen Manor and back.
4 miles.**

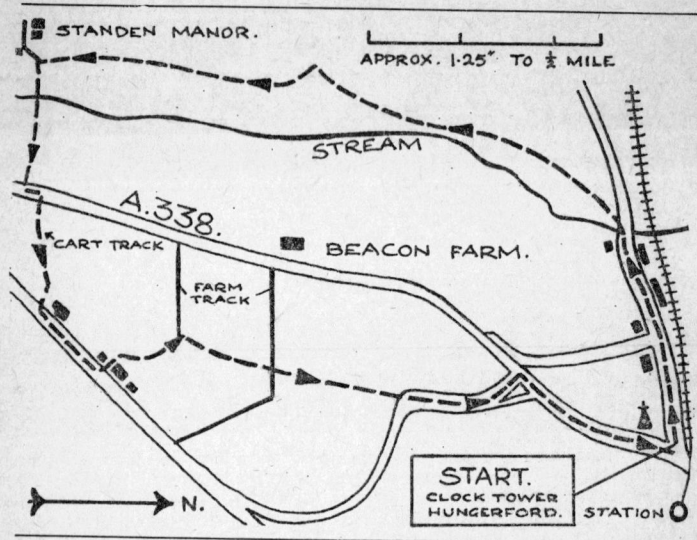

Once the town is behind you these paths travel through countryside which is surprisingly remote. It is open agricultural land, both arable and pasture, where you may well flush up a pheasant or a covey of partridge, and certainly hear the call of the restless peewits. A not-over-strenuous walk, which might be muddy here and there in winter, it is best enjoyed at a leisurely pace.

How to get there—By car to car park in Church Street, just off middle of High Street.

By train to Hungerford.

By bus: Thames Valley 113 Newbury-Hungerford, and

other services. Alight at Clock Tower.

For this and the next Hungerford walk I have taken as the first landmark the distinctive Clock Tower in the High Street.

So, from the Clock Tower walk up Church Street, passing the Fire Station and the Angel. Ahead, ignoring turnings off, for approximately ½ mile stay with road as it bends right past the Great Western Mills, and crosses a small stream. Here go left over stile and as P.F. sign points. Cross meadow to find and cross a stile. Ahead again, across field to meet corner of hedge and an inconspicuous P.F. sign.

Keep straight on, hedge left, and when field ends discover stile a yard or two to your right. Climb, forward for few yards only, to second stile. Immediately make a right-hand turn over a third stile and cross narrow field to two further stiles in quick succession.

Now turn left, and follow the lower edge of an extensive field till eventually you reach a gate. Beyond it the buildings of Standen Manor are glimpsed forward right. But the path is forward slightly left over the pasturage to stile and P.F. sign. Here turn left along surfaced driveway and after ¼ mile arrive at road (A338).

Turn left along the grass verge for 20 yards then cross road to take cart track facing you. A further ¼ mile on it brings you to a quiet by-road. Go left along it for rather less than ¼ mile, where turn left via gate as a P.F. sign indicates.

You are on a track which winds right behind farm buildings, then goes ahead, initially with wooden fencing and then fine mixed hedgerow right. When farm track makes a definite left turn, leave it and carry on forward in line with right edge of field. At far right hand corner emerge on to another farm track, cross, and with a low hedgerow right and line of telegraph poles right, continue ahead to road.

By keeping forward with road, it will take you back down to Hungerford.

Refreshments The Coffee House and Coffee Lounge in Hungerford Arcade, both in High Street.

Hungerford

**Hungerford Common, Templeton,
Dun Mill Lock.
4 miles.**

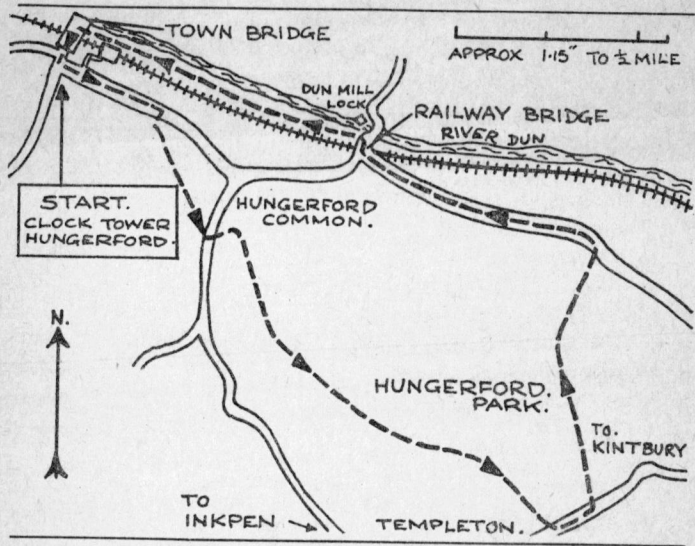

This is an interesting walk, encountering few stiles, but with level and varied paths crossing both common and pastoral land, and returning via the picturesque Dun Mill and along the towpath. I have suggested Hungerford town as the starting point, but it is also possible to park on Hungerford Common and pick up walk at (A) (i.e. Park Street entrance to Common).

How to get there—As Walk 18.

From the Clock Tower cross the High Street and walk up Park Street opposite. Once past turning left to station—there is a pavement—simply go straight on, and past gate and cattle grid on to Hungerford Common.

(A) On the Common leave road, and bear right to go diagonally across the grass till you arrive at road with further gate and grid. Cross road. Walk diagonally left for a few steps (fencing right), then turn right to carry on down to stile in far right-hand corner of Common. Climb, and immediately over a second. Then, having woodland left initially, bear left beside edge of large field to gate at far side. Beyond it, cross gravel track, and forward over pastureland, hedge left, downs in distance right.

When larch plantation occurs left, still ahead. On it ceasing, simply continue forward till you meet a hedgerow. Turn right for 30 yards then left through a wide gap into next field. From here go slightly right—path tends to be faint—to visible long gate in distant hedge. This leads you on to road at Templeton.

Turn left for 100 yards, and just past Templeton Stud go left again on public bridleway (Private Road). Soon passing a couple of houses, stay with this broad clear roadway for nearly a mile as it skirts the grounds of Hungerford Park.

When you emerge on road turn left along it to soon pass the lodge and main gates to the house. A short way on re-reach the Common, beside the usual gate and grid. Straight ahead over the Common, in line with road.

The next landmark is the railway bridge. Walk across it as if to Lower Denford, and follow road round to speedily arrive at Dun Mill Lock, where turn left to follow the towpath, i.e. keeping on left bank, though you may well want to pause here awhile, as this is a very attractive corner beside the River Dun.

Walk along the towpath, crossing over stile opposite the Mill, and stay with it till a white wooden bridge is reached. Note the typical canal hedge, basically quickthorn amongst which a whole variety of bramble, elder, field maple, wild rose and other shrubs have intermingled.

At the bridge, go round it, and on beside canal, to quickly arrive at the brick Town Bridge, where the duck love to congregate. Now go left up to the High Street, and by continuing forward you will re-reach the Clock Tower.

Kintbury

**Kennet and Avon Canal, Titcomb Manor,
Mount Pleasant, Kintbury Crossways.
3½ miles.**

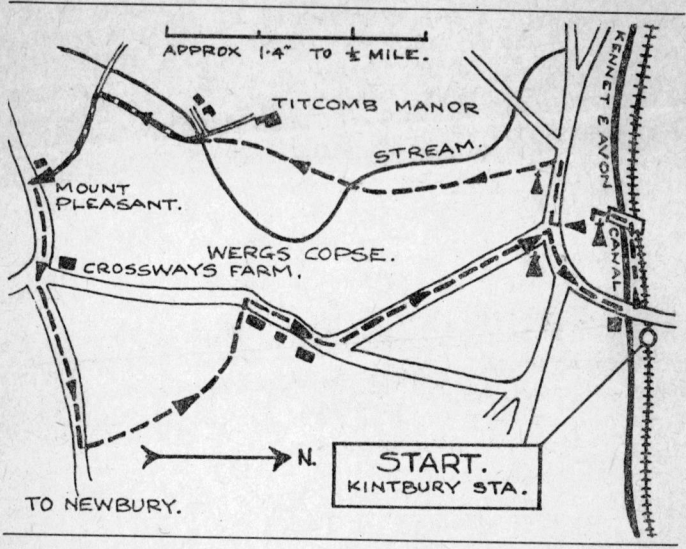

This, the last of these walks around Berkshire, is a short excursion along the paths and quiet lanes south of Kintbury. In walking such Berkshire lanes we have discovered that one of their notable characteristics is that many of them, wandering past, or to, a solitary farm or manorial house perhaps, are often as rural and pleasant to walk along as the footpaths.

A settlement was known to be here in Saxon times, and the old part of the historic village is well worth exploring. It was known to Jane Austen, who stayed here with her sister on several occasions.

How to get there—By car, and park by either station or church.
By train to Kintbury (B.R.) No service on Sundays.

By bus: Thames Valley 113 Newbury to Hungerford—infrequent. Alight in Station Road, Kintbury.

Kintbury, just east of Hungerford, is one of those rare villages which still boasts a live station on the Reading to Westbury line. So what better place to start the walk than the station?

Turn towards the Dundas Arms, and walk a step or two to reach the Kennet and Avon Canal, it runs alongside the railway, as is so often the case.

Do not cross the canal, but go right along the towpath. There is usually a line of boats moored to the opposite bank below the lovely old Mill house, and coot, mallard and swans are regular inhabitants of these waters. Continue till just short of a mellow, brick bridge, where, having observed how well it compares with the utilitarian one over the railway, leave the canal bank by walking up clear path ahead.

At the top turn left over the canal bridge, and keep ahead up a brick path into the churchyard. Go on past the church to emerge at the far side in Church Street.

Kintbury church, though much restored, has traces of Norman architecture, notably the south doorway.

To continue, walk on up Church Street. On meeting the shops at a cross-roads, turn right along the High Street, to reach the Blue Ball.

Over a century ago, in 1830, when agricultural labourers rose up in protest against low wages and other hardships, some of the ring leaders were arrested at the Blue Ball, which was used as their local headquarters.

Immediately beyond the inn, turn left up Titcomb Way. Within a few yards follow the P.F. ahead. At first the path is narrowly confined, but it speedily widens out to become a well-used cart track. Slightly sunken, and increasingly well-hedged, it is a sheltered track and I recommend coming this way in late autumn especially to see the slender branches of the spindle tree bright with delicate, cyclamen-pink fruit.

Follow the track forward till eventually you meet a metal kissing-gate. Go through, and along much narrower path edging grazing land, and very soon cross a little bridge over the right-hand ditch. At this stage a hedged path takes you on;

should it appear slightly overgrown, don't be disheartened, it is of short duration, and you soon emerge into open meadowland.

Walk forward on green path towards visible house. Follow path, bearing left to skirt the grounds of Titcomb Manor, so that, passing a row of trees and holly right, you come out to a lane by a P.F. sign. Turn left along lane, away from house, thus crossing a streamlet. Soon winding round, stay with lane as it rises gently to a road junction at Mount Pleasant. You will find the name on a post-box just to right. But our way is left.

Carry on till you arrive at a cross-roads, by Crossways Farm. Go straight over, and ahead as signposted to Newbury. After nearly $\frac{1}{2}$ mile find a high stile on your left ushering you into meadowland again. Go on, wire fence left. Half-way over cross a farm track, and continue down to wood. At the bottom you have to perform a minor athletic feat by crossing a couple of stiles, with a solid plank over a ditch between them.

From here keep forward up right edge of meadow, and at top right-hand corner find, what I can only describe as an awkward stile. Negotiate it as best you can, and then make your way up over the grass and between bracken, curving left to emerge on to a wide farm track. Cross it to a makeshift stile leading into a field.

Walk towards left of two houses, and at further side of field go down a narrow pathway between a house and a bungalow. This brings you to road, and a P.F. sign confirms you're on the right route. Turn right along road, and when it forks take left fork (signposted to Hungerford) which will take you to Station Road, Kintbury. Turn right to return to the station. And, just before you reach it looking left you will see a line of stepping stones leading to the Mill House; an unusual sight in Berkshire.

Refreshments Inns in Kintbury.